THE WEATHER

THE WEATHER

LORNA CROZIER

COTEAU BOOKS

Some of these poems have been broadcast on CBC radio on "Anthology" and "Ambience" and have appeared in the following magazines: *Saturday Night, Event, Fireweed, NeWest ReView, Branching Out, Writers' News Manitoba, Malahat Review, Northern Light, Fiddlehead, Dandelion, Grain, South Dakota Review, Poetry Canada Review, Moosehead Review, Canadian Dimension,* and *Fort Sanity.*

Cover drawing and design and inside drawings by Jane Turnbull Evans.
Photograph by Richard Gustin.
Produced by First Impressions Ltd.

We gratefully acknowledge the assistance of the Saskatchewan Arts Board, the Canada Council, and the City of Regina in the publication of this book.

The author would like to thank the Poets' Combine for their advice, Patrick Lane for his continuing faith and encouragement, and Lise Perrault for her translation which inspired the poem "The First Woman". She would also like to thank the Saskatchewan Writers/Artists Colonies and the Southwest Writers' Project in Swift Current for the year's residency which allowed her time to write.

Canadian Catologuing in Publication Data

Crozier, Lorna, 1948 —
    The weather
Poems.
ISBN 0-919926-23-1 (bound). — ISBN 0-919926-24-X (pbk.)

I. Title.
PS8555.R72W4 1983   C811'.54   C83-091388-2
PR9199.3.C76W4 1983

40, 702

coteau books

Thunder Creek Publishing Co-operative Limited
Box 239, Sub. #1
Moose Jaw, Saskatchewan S6H 5V0

For the Croziers, whose name
I have reclaimed.

I'd like to live a slower life.
The weather gets in my words
and I want them dry. Line after line
writes itself on my face, not a grace
of age but wrinkled humour.

John Newlove

Table of Contents

Section One

Section Two

Section Three

Section Four

SECTION ONE

The Apple Tree

1.

The apple tree hums
white blossoms turn
yellow, honey bees carry
the shape of tree
up up in a buzzing
bloom high into the
high wind

2.

How beautiful
the muted birds
as if a delicate finger
smudged the colours
into a haze, a grey whisper
the cedar waxwings dart
among branches
like leaf shadows moved
by wind they flutter
oh beautiful the birds
that feed on blossoms

3.

Wind breathes through
the tree, loosens petals
into a butterfly's
brief flight
       they light
from birth to death
in a wing instant, a
sigh, the petals fall
— white silk rain

4.

Someone says
       it's just like a wedding
       this white confetti
and we laugh
none of us believing
in weddings anymore
still we sit
where petals
settle in our hair
blessings
in the early
apple morning

The Weather

I want to wade in liquid heat,
submerge in the light
where all things are possible:
black birds turn iridescent,
finches flicker like candles
from green to green.
I want to believe in you.
I want your hands
to carry the sun to our bed.

Instead the cold follows us
like an old wrong we can't undo.
Christ, it's summer, we say,
thinking the word
will make it happen.

Even our faith in seasons
is misplaced. A hand moves across
a pencil drawing of the world
and smudges everything.

The Foetus Dreams

1.

Lungs.
It dreams heart.
Spleen. Liver.
It dreams two faces:

one it will wear
before it is born.

2.

In the morning
the foetus dreams the sun.
It pushes against red walls
wanting to touch light
with pale buds of fingers.

There is no sun.

The foetus dreams
the shadow of a cloud
bruises its eyelids.
It hears rain
tapping on the forehead
of its mother.
It dreams
it is a fish that swims
in her laughter
through the seasons
of her blood.

3.

The foetus dreams
wind fills its skin-bag,
lifts it out and up

an ocular *o*

round and clear
as a bubble blown
from a child's ring.

The earth shrinks
to a speck of dust
under a new-formed nail.
Stars like fireflies
catch in its fine
black hair.

4.

The foetus dreams
it is a whisper
sealed in a clear jar
set on a kitchen shelf
where a red geranium
presses its petals
against glass skin
until night turns
the window cold and dark.

5.

The foetus dreams a man
hangs a moonstone around its mother's throat.

It dreams a man
follows her through the shadows of the park,

stands outside her bedroom window,
leaves his breath in circles on the pane.

It dreams a man with a face it has known
moves his mouth in words across her belly.

It cries and kicks
                    the voice away
beating the stretched skin like a drum.

6.

The foetus dreams a name
it fills like a round
glass or a mouth.
It moves like light
into the spaces defined
by the letters. It moves
like breath into the spaces
between the letters.

It grows within the name
as ice expands in stone
fissures
            yet the stone holds
and will not break.

7.

The foetus dreams it is
a black hole
             cut into the tinny blue.
It dreams someone
cuts off its foot for a dime,
someone splits its tongue
so it can say a word. It dreams
it sits on its mother's hip
while she lies sleeping. In the dawn
it flies away
             with her black
and dreaming eyes.

8.

It dreams it is a mouth,
a fish swimming in a mouth.
It dreams its mother
hooks a fish.
She reels it in
on a long thin vein
she winds
round and round her wrist.

9.

The foetus dreams it is a man.
It dreams it is a woman.
It dreams it is half
                and half.
It dreams it is unhappy.
It dreams two pains: one
will not stop after the foetus
squeezes from the vise,
the tight tunnel.

It wants to be
a thing with wings
that says one word
                over and over.

10.

The woman turns in sleep,
the foetus turns. She dreams
a thing inside her.
It eats her heart.
It chews through her belly.
It splits her in two
like an avocado, a stone
rolls out. It is a fish
with teeth, a bird with spurs,
a plant that roots in her lungs.
It rides out of her
on a black horse,
it cries *Mother*.

The Child Who Walks Backwards

My next-door neighbour tells me
her child runs into things.
Cupboard corners and doorknobs
have pounded their shapes
into his face. She says
he is bothered by dreams,
rises in sleep from his bed
to steal through the halls
and plummet like a wounded bird
down the flight of stairs.

This child who climbed my maple
with the sureness of a cat,
trips in his room, cracks
his skull on the bedpost,
smacks his cheeks on the floor.
When I ask about the burns
on the back of his knee,
his mother tells me
he walks backwards
into fireplace grates
or sits and stares at flames
while sparks burn stars in his skin.

Other children write their names
on the casts that hold
his small bones.
His mother tells me
he runs into things,
walks backwards,
breaks his leg
while she lies
sleeping.

Letter to a Lover Far From Home

Outside my window the birds are silent.
Soon they will awaken as light touches
the leaves. The country where they go
when our green sinks into earth
lives inside their sleeping:
the bougainvillea, limes and lemons,
the brown-skinned people you walk among now.

Perhaps it is the birds
who see you walking in the sun,
who dream the face I have forgotten.
When it was winter here
they watched you in the plaza,
writing letters home in the long afternoons.
You paused
when you saw familiar wings
and listened to them sing your cold country.

Here it is spring.
The birds have returned to our trees
and day is breaking. As you walk
to the marketplace, the sun
that warms your face
slips through my curtains.

This is all to say:
such singing there will be
when you return.

This is a Love Poem Without Restraint

This poem
is full of pain
full of pieces
It cries out
oh! oh! oh!
It has no pride
no discretion
It whimpers
It will not drop its eyes
when it meets a stranger
It will not hide
its tears

    •

It will talk
of beauty
Lilacs Apples
The smell of rain
in caraganas
Your mouth
your eyes

What are you going to do about it?
You cannot stop me
now

    •

The moon shines on this page
as the poem writes
itself. It is trying to find
whiteness
frost on snow
two feathers
on a pillow
your hands
        upon
my skin

   •

These words are tired
of being
        words
They refuse to sit here
pretending
        they can't move
                off the page

These are the first
ones to leave
their white space
They fall
on your tongue
letter
        by
           letter
like raindrops

One of them
is my name

What will you do with it?
It has decided to live
inside you

   •

This poem has no restraint
It will not say
plum blossom
sunset
rubbing stone
cat's cradle

It refuses to be evasive

I miss you
I miss you
Come home

•

It won't talk of passion
but the sleep that follows
when our bodies
touch

that moment
just before waking
when we realize
we've been holding one another
in our sleep

•

How do you use the word *love*
in a poem?

Love.

If you look at it
long enough
it will burn into your eyes
and last

Pavlova

Even you, Pavlova, you
with the beautiful feet and arms,
even you did not die
with grace or beauty.
Your last words
Get my swan costume ready
were what we would have written
for you, but death would not
lift you weightless
into the bright air.

You waited
in the shadows of the wings,
moistening your lips,
crossing yourself as you had
a hundred times before.
Should I have had children instead?
Sons and daughters
to show pictures to.
This is the country I left,
see why I weep.

In Russia the snow is falling
as it does in memory, falling
on the backs of horses,
settling in the furs of women
who ride to the concert halls.
In your garden in England
the swan who laid his neck
across your shoulders
and bit your flesh
in his dark unpredictable beak
dreams himself whole again
up to where the sky
was made for swans.

Lonely and sick you lie
in a Dutch hotel.
Your lungs like stones
press you into the bed.
Clutching your husband's hand,
you feel the warmth of the mistress
he left just moments ago,
hear his words
She will not dance tomorrow,
as the doctor cuts
into your ribcage
to drain the pus
and let the breath in.

Children of Dream

My children are thin,
thin as bands of light
from under closed doors.
Their skin transparent,
I can read the blue
scrawl of veins
the small clenched hearts,
see the animals who sleep
inside their wide foreheads.

I want to give them words
the blind must know:
bell   snow
tongue   pain,
want to explain
innocence, its loss,
love, its many failures.

Instead my refrain
is what they'll see:
the slight shift of colour
in stubble fields, the light
spilling from a magpie's wing,
if they would only open
their eyes to the morning.

They stay behind doors,
children of dreams,
eloquent and sightless
in the upstairs room.

Mid-February

Outside the grey sky
falls and continues to fall
around your muffled body
that bends, straightens, bends,
your dull blade bruising wood.

In the frame of the window
a bird lights on the dying elm.
Its breast is bright, yellow
as the three chrysanthemums
you brought home yesterday
wrapped in tissue and waxed paper
green as growing.

Through flowers I watch
your red mitts following
the axe, the image of the bird
held in glass. I cup
the colours to my eyes
to wash away the hours
when I couldn't show my care
or feel the simple joy
of flowers and a bird.

As you pile wood
in the crook of your arm,
the bird stretches its wings.
Up from the warm throat
its song rises in the snow,
in the slow heart.

Eclipse

Last night they came to visit.
One talked of women who dance
with balding men, wiggle
their asses to attract
those who sit
backs to the wall.
These new women
want to be blessed
with blood. They want men
who put their balls in glass
cases on display.

The other talked of rape,
men who turn
icons to the wall,
hold boiling water
above the woman's face
until she opens. *A fantasy,*
for a film about the prairies.

This morning my lover and I
walk to the river to see the eclipse,
the last of this century, the last
before we die. We hold hands, watch
the joining of sun and moon.
A bat, thinking it is night,
stumbles into the sky.

What the Mind Turns Over

What the mind turns over
and over like polished stones
are the blue butterflies
rising from grass
as we passed the altars.

At Uzmal we listened
to the old stories:
the butterflies are souls
of those the priests
tore open, hearts beating
high in the sun. The ruins
are memories now, here
where snow drifts by the windows.

Across the room shadows
touch your face.
Wings open and close
like fragile hands,
delicate as frost
forming on glass.

As you fall asleep,
they brush my skin,
settle in my hair.
Nothing that moves
is so blue.

Beneath Our Feet

Beneath our feet the gopher
in his earth tunnel
waits for us to pass
before he searches for seeds.

You walk beside me. Shadows
repeat the shapes of trees,
how they sway across the grass.
My shadow darkens your face.
You are silent, removed
from my words, the touch
of my fingers.

What caves do you move through?
Will you find a pool
lit by a pillar of sun
or will you find a darkness
so deep at the centre
that all you believe
falls away?

The gopher stands on his hind legs
like a little man and watches us go.
He is made for the close hug of earth.
See his sleek body, his ears
pressed flat against his head
like fragile shells.

I want to call you
to the sun, call you away
from silences and caves.
Birds fly up, take us with them
as we pass. See how all the light
flows around us.

SECTION TWO

Wild Geese

The wild geese fly
the same pathways
they have followed for centuries.

There is comfort in this
though they are not the same
geese my mother listened to
when she was young.

Perhaps I first heard them
inside her
as she watched their wings
eclipse the moon, their call
the first sound — separate
from the soft, aquatic
whispers of the womb.

And my sadness is her sadness
passed through generations
like distance and direction
and the longing
for the nesting ground.

Between Seasons

It is mid-May but the blossoms
remain inside the apple tree.
Clouds hang over the valley
like stained and matted wool
nothing can break through.
And the wife of my friend
has left him.

I watch him mend his jeans,
as he did when she was there,
but now his attention
to the needle and the thread
has a special sadness.

The patches, the red stitches
will save the jeans for one more season
though the seasons merge like years
that have lost their edges,
or faces we barely remember
that meant everything once.

Only the thread is bright and clear —
brave, uneven hyphens of colour
joining him precariously
to the morning.

Rain

So many write of rain
its small hands,
the memories it brings,
the sounds of things it touches.

How it changes what we see,
gives taste to what we thought
was tasteless: the grey of morning,
love's failures, the simple fear
of growing old
alone.

I think of this
as you drive away.
In the blacktop mirror
you are leaving
in the rain
you are leaving.

Your taillights burn
holes in the night
rain fills and spills from,
changing everything
except the songs
it carries to the earth.

Spring Storm, 1916

1.

Cleat McLeod saw
the storm coming
He wrapped his arms
around the stall post
and yelled to his wife
running for the root cellar
> *If the barn goes*
> *I go with it*

He and the post
were ten feet off the ground
before he could let go

2.

The south edge of the cyclone
lifted Teman Leep's
new hip-roofed barn
Wind and land
clapped their hands together
smashed the building flat

The old tumble-down house
his wife wished would fall
stood firm

3.

The wind lifted
Prine Gossard's house
so all the furniture
       slid to one side

Granny Gossard
rode her rocking chair
right through the parlour window
She only broke a leg

4.

Shorty Turnbull refused
to stop plowing
His hired hand ran
to the rock pile
       (later over a beer
         in Stanley Buck's basement
         he said *First time I've*
         ever been thankful
         for a rock)
and hung on

The wind lifted
horse, man and plow
set them in Sylvester's field
seven miles away

Turnbull plowed his neighbour's
quarter section
before he knew
where he was

27

5.

On the way down the cellar
Esther Simmie's new
store-bought hat
blew back East
where it came from

Next year, a storm
blew in from the opposite direction
Her husband caught the hat
as it sailed by the house

6.

Everyone lived to tell
even the old Dutchman's wife
who was struck by lightning
(the only woman for miles
so lonely
she followed his plow like a dog)

She wasn't killed
but she's walked stooped ever since

7.

Chickens were lifted up
like cottonwood fluff
and gently lowered
to the east of the yard

After that taste of flying
those hens never laid good again
but kept on flapping
blunt wings
like headless chickens
trying to rise above
their own blood

8.

Like an animal compelled
to return and tear apart
the cage that held it
the wind
doubled the windmill tower
like a wishbone
and planted its blades
in the dark mud

9.

The Model T
never moved

Riding the Borders of the Land

Riding behind Steve on the mare
I hold his waist, the broad
leather belt. Around us
the sky is dark, thunder
rolls from the horizon.
He shows me where
his land begins and ends,
talks of leaving.
It's a hard life:
drought for two years,
the fences need mending
and if he doesn't pull down
the old barn soon
it will fall in the next strong wind,
boards breaking like stubble
under the horse's hooves.

I think of Liz who followed him
from New Zealand, the poems
that tear from her, working their way
through her heart like quills.
But this year's going to be good,
Steve says and laughs. *The barley's*
thick and green as money.
He pulls on the reins
as the mare begins to trot.
She is Liz's horse, not used to
his grip, she wants to run.

By the house Liz waits for us
in the dust. She wishes
the land in four directions
was ocean, blue and green
as the bits of glass
hung in all her windows.
She crosses the yard, milk pails
banging against her legs.
The rain begins, gentle at first.
Soon it is a wall we break through,
the horse running.

Liz leans into the cow.
Above the sound of milk
thrumming into the pail,
she hears gulls, their cries
circling the weather vane.
The barn begins to creak.
Like an old boat
it sways in the rain,
the day's last wind.

Ancestry
(for Sara and Eli)

Sara the young one
born in the city
hears his confession
> *It was the wind*
> *When I left the prairie*
> *I pulled it from the sky*
> *buried it*
> *like a grandfather*
> *you have never seen*

That summer they return
to the graves of their ancestors
Her father walks among stones
among gravehouses   reads aloud
the Hebraic letters
writes them down in books

Sara finds the marker
washed nameless by rain
unearths the old bones
scrapes them clean
with a xyster   zt   zt   zt
draws a mouth on the skull
She sees the grasses move
feels invisible
fingers ruffle her hair

In a paper bag
she carries them
back to the city
strings them together
hangs them in her window
At night they chime
the names of all her dead
and what they have seen of the dark
wind in the marrow
wind in the heart

Woman from the West Coast

The beautiful one   the woman
who wears long flowered skirts
that cling to her legs
as if the wind were water
tells me that what I call sage
is not.
> *It's witch's moss*
> *I grow it in my garden*
> *have for years.*

She is an expert. She's read
all the names in books
and uses herbs to make
her spells. In an almanac
she records shapes of the moon
times of tides and planting.

I have lived on the prairie
all my life   have rubbed
the silver-green of sage
into my skin   crushed the leaves
into my hair   laid them
on the eyelids of my lover.
I wonder what
she'll call the wind.

Drought

The hawk sits on the post,
head tucked in his shoulder.
It is mid-day. He knows the sun,
if he took flight, would singe
his wings and burn the moisture
from his eyes. Around him mice
crackle through the yellow grass,
their bodies small flames. Gophers
driven by the memory of seeds
move from darkness.

The hawk sleeps,
head tucked in his shoulder.
Soon he must hunt,
slice his wings through heat
that beats like rain
on the dry earth. His shadow
will offer the small
        a moment's respite
before he drops and drinks
long and deep.

Fall

10,000 snow geese, he says
I've never seen anything like it
as if a cloud had opened up
emptied all its down into the lake
making it a soft white bed
for you and me to love on

       three snow geese
       on the kitchen table
       heads and necks hang
       over the edge, ice
       pendulums in broken clocks
       drip drip drip
       bright seconds counted out

see what I've brought you
goose for our supper
feathers for your dreams

Tigers

What do you do with the names,
Siberian, Himalayan, Bengal?
Words to hang old fears upon.

Do tigers born in zoos
believe in tigers anymore?
Do they fall into themselves,
smell their wild blood
        and remember
a green so violent
it burns in their eyes.

At night ivy and violets
spill from clay pots,
flood the room with leaves.
Around the dark house
Himalayan, Siberian, Bengal
stalk the edges of your sleep,
the fall of their padded feet
muffled by your breath.
Now they are the same
colour as night, a deep blue
moving at the corners of your eyes,
stretching lithe shadows along the branches.

Your fears rise to meet them
like a friend meets another
who has come from a time and place
so far away
the name is remembered
only when the hands touch.

There Are Limits

He has a present for me,
something he caught
this morning in Echo Lake.
I think of the lure,
the dead eyes.
A fish? I ask.
Better than that, he replies,
pulling from his pocket
a piece of glass
shaped like a fish.

He presses it into my palm,
tells me he'll stop
thinking of me now.
He has reeled in
his line, the fish
is made of glass.
Life is not what we thought
there are limits
to loving.

I hang the glass
by a thread in my window.
It turns and turns
tangling the sunlight,
echoes of fish
flicker on the walls.

This is better than a word,
better than a promise.
There are limits to giving.

Last Day of Fall
(for Howie White)

The wind cold, the cold wind
bringing in tomorrow's frost.
Flower beds dug up, the soil turned,
and in the yellow grass that was not cut
in the last few days of growing, a bird
hunches, then hops lopsided away:
bird with one wing dragging, beautiful
russet breast, a beak to gather seeds.

The last sweet moments of fall
we wanted to gather in, gold leaves
to carry us through the winter.
Instead a broken bird at our feet
and what's to be done?
Let it die slowly in a box or cage?
Kill it here? This is the last day
of fall. In nights that grow longer
a bird will drag its wing across our eyes.

Somewhere there is a man
who can kill. Neither of us can
strike it with a stone or crush
its skull with our heels.
We turn away, leave it in the grass.
Here there are seeds, we say,
the euthanasia of early snow,
the quick mercy
of a cat.

South Dakota Refuge

Go to Sand Lake, she says,
in November it's a platter
full of geese, your geese,
the Canadas come down with the snow,
feed on marsh grass
before their Southern flight.

Along the border of the refuge:
wind off the lake, grey fog settling
on the water, the stir of wings.
Men warm their hands on thermoses,
cigarettes burn the morning air.
Against the cars like young boys,
bored, waiting for the end of silence,
the guns lean.

Study in Grey

The great horned owl unrolls
her last long vowel to the tallow moon.
She abandons shadows, the light
and half-light of poplars around the empty house,
the broken plows and crockery,
the windmill that does not turn the wind.
No longer will she watch you search
through dust for pictures of your past.
She has seen her shadow nailed to the barn
and her young die in eggs that have no shells.

In White

The snowy owl flies
to the place where snow begins.
Only those pale as winter have survived:
the albino wolf, the sleek and silver fox.
But even where snow turns
everything to silence
and stills time like mercury
frozen in glass, she is not safe.
Across the moving ice
the white hunter drives his huskies
into her amber eyes.

Winter Morning

Wake up you say
I have something
to show you

I cross
the cold linoleum
to the window

Three deer
nibble
on the apple tree

Their breath
thaws frost
from branches

Snow melts
as it touches
their backs

The last winter
we were together

three doe
met our eyes
not afraid

you on my left
in the morning light
and I

already leaving
as the deer turned
from frozen buds

to follow their tracks
one by one
across the snow

Magpie

Red willow
and raspberry canes,
frost on the bright morning.

Outside my window a magpie
shakes white from his wings,
warns the day

I am stepping out.

The Whistling Swans Are Gone

The whistling swans are gone,
the sandpipers, the Canada geese
pull spring farther north.
Mallards and teal no longer
find ponds in ditches
like bits of broken mirror.

In the house the farmer
stands at the western window.
Dust covers the glass
like curtains of torn lace.
The woman turns plates
upside-down on the breakfast table
and children,
remembering old stories,
step on spiders that spin
in dark corners of the room.

In the fields cows move slowly.
Even the slow, the mute animals
dream of green, of cool mud
by the willows where clouds
brush the earth with shadows,
then drift from sight,
ghosts of great white swans.

Albino Bull

The white bull of legend
grazed with the herds
on the plains, a dreamspirit
rising from shaggy heads.
His nose touched the buttocks
of the favoured cows,
young and fat, pale calves
stirring inside them.

He was the leader, the hunted one
worth more than guns and whiskey.
There were stories of bullets
just missing
and stories of blizzards
when the old bull led hunters
in circles through the snow
until they were covered by a white robe
and none were found in spring.

Legends named him Big Medicine,
Buffalo of the Sun,
and men believed in his power,
his existence beyond story.

Now when the herds no longer
rove across the prairies
and it's difficult to believe
in anything
I will call the white bull
Buffalo of the Moon
and believe thousands of his calves
roam the lunar plains
turning the dark side white.

SECTION THREE

The First Woman

The first white woman in the West
Marie Anne Lagimodière
born 1782
she did exist
her reality stops me

who am I to tell
her story?
what is it
I want to know?

I am not the first
white woman in the West
I am not Catholic
I am not French
but in this wilderness
I cross
I am the first
woman   these words
          my signs
for those
who went before

He was a voyageur come back
to Trois-Rivières
every night he told stories
all of us come to listen
and who cares
            it was not the truth
but exciting

his voice rose
and fell with the fire
shadows in the room
were Indians
            or wild animals
that tore us apart
if we leaned too far back
in our chairs

when he proposed
I never thought
            of asking
if he would stay
in the village
nor did my father
everyone so sure
he wasn't thinking
of wandering again
all those stories
death and the long wind
that had no trees
to stop it

but a month after the wedding
he was pulled by spring
onto the rivers
                and me
what was I to do?
not young   twenty-five
become a housekeeper
for Father Vinet
or go with him?

The first man to cross this river
to climb this hill   to write
his name in stone
the first man to be held
in the eyes of a doe
that did not know
to run

did these stories
draw you to him?
or while others listened
did you feel desire?
watch the gestures
of his hands, his face
his lean body moving
through your eyes
through the village
that was the world

After the water
I didn't mind the trip
so much
but the canoes
they were dangerous

on Lake Superior   no need
for tales of monsters
wind and wave rose
from the cold
with foaming mouths
we rowed from bay to bay
praying in between

the canoe just ahead
flipped over   men thrashed
grasping the air
for the hand of God
                    grown men
crying for *Mary*   for their mothers

sucked down
                into the black
cold belly of the lake

I bruised my palm
clutching the beads
so tight

These things protect you
  : the holy beads
  : God
  : a fire
  : the single-shot
   rifle
  : your husband

but he keeps changing
      shape
he is a wolf
a lynx a muskrat
a weasel a cougar
a silver fox
filling your doorway
after the long season

Sitting around the fire
Bouvier on the other side
screams *Mon Dieu*
Mon Dieu this is just
across the fire   we think
it can't be animals
the fire makes us safe
my husband grabs his rifle
we see a bear sow
drag Bouvier into the bush
Shoot   shoot
Don't let me be eaten alive

she batters his head
my husband clubs her
with his rifle   fires
she drops her prey
rears at him
he runs for his other gun
the bullet strikes
she does not rise again

no screams   no words
just gargling sounds
from Bouvier
            the bear has torn off
his face as if it were a mask
nose eyes mouth all gone

What remains when the fire
no longer holds back the fear
when the gun will not go off
when the healing herbs are poison
what remains?

beads to bruise the palm
the words of the priest from the lost village
the man who sleeps with you
under the skins of what he has killed
the living cooking washing mending
saying your prayers
praying

       little enough
but enough to keep you going

when Indians try to buy your child
and your husband moves
from trap to trap
           across the snow

It was the custom
you know
but he never told me
he took a squaw
the four years he stayed
at Pembina

and this woman was kind
she visits me every day
shows me herbs for healing
tells me with her hands
she'll make a drink
to take away the weakness
I've carried
since the first baby

she helps me
with the hides
shows me how
to scrape away the flesh
how to rub the liver
brains and fat into the skin
for a jacket
that will please him

her knife goes *snik snik*
across the surface
I am clumsy
leave spots of blood
like cricket tracks
across wet clay

she gestures
        soon she'll have this drink
for me

I speak only French
she Blackfoot
hands shape our thoughts in the air
hers are dusty swallows
she wants to tell me
    my husband will like
    this skin we work on

when she forms the word
for *husband*
      I know
she has known him
as only a wife can

and I do not take the drink

While an Indian wife waited at Pembina
softening his skins with her spittle
he returned to the village he left behind
married a woman of his kind

did he desire
                your piety?
your very name *Marie* his mother's
his sister's   memories one needs
to press into the heart
when the canoe tips over
the gun jams   a bear grows out of fire

did he want you
                    to stay in the village
until he returned old and tired
his children strangers   his wife
a grey woman to pray away his sins?

but you demanded
to go with him
                    the first white woman
the Indians had seen
worth many horses hides and guns

you waited
at the end of the trapline
hands that worried beads
touching the images you shaped of him
in the dark unholy hours

Never in one place long
by spring he wants to go
this time
        to Fort of the Prairies

from an Indian trader
he buys me a horse
a good one   gentle
but strong for a long journey

by twilight we crest a hill
a herd of buffalo
grazes in the valley
my horse stiffens
too late I know
he's a buffalo runner
throws himself
          down the hill
splits the herd
buffalo explode around us
my horse running
        running

later   on the saddle blanket
that stinks of dust and sweat
the new baby tears from me
           rips me in two
flies settle on his head
       I name him
Laprairie

Twelve years
of following your husband
from place to place

until the priests arrive
at Red River
they build a church
your husband builds
a house from wood

> bells divide time
> into hours and years

at the bedside
he asks you to keep
his gun
his leather jacket
hangs on a nail
beside the door
until your son
packs it away

you blow sparks
in the black stove
stack pieces of wood
around a weak flame

Would I have lived otherwise?
what a question
              of course
I would have had a priest
to baptize the children
a mother near
a father   uncles   cousins
sisters   a village and trees
old as the land

people who shared
              my tongue
fires built only for warmth
and the closeness of stories
a husband
who did not think
he was a river
who didn't think
he had to fill the sky
or stretch his shadow
                        so far
across the snow

but then
I could have married a village boy
covered with dirt from the fields
ah   who knows
              who knows
would I have lived otherwise?

I lived   I had children
I am old

Sharing this place
you call *desert*
outside of the country
you came from
country old enough
to have a name
                    Canada

sharing this body
this human fear
                    of being
alone
        of living
in another's house

this made you
leave the known behind
                    I leave
what I know
like strips of red cotton
tied to branches

if you listen   first woman
you will hear the steps
of one who follows
far in the back of your mind
moving out towards your eyes

SECTION FOUR

The Women Who Survive

My mother and my aunt
talk of disaster
they are that old now
they talk of death
every morning over coffee
the same dark chant

Scotty MacKay, you know him, he's the third uncle of your cousin
twice removed, perfectly healthy man, went down the basement to
change the filter in the furnace, when he didn't come up for supper,
his wife went down and found him dead.
Remember Alf Tone, my aunt says, I'm sure he was murdered,
they found him in the cistern where he'd been for two months.
Not murdered, says my mother, he was probably just cleaning it
and his heart gave out.
No, he had his going-to-town clothes on, no one cleans the cistern
with their going-to-town clothes on.

It's always the men
who die, they keel over
at the breakfast table
breaking poached eggs
with their foreheads
or they fall in the shower
clutching ropes of water
that refuse to hold them

So unexpected, say
my mother and my aunt
nibbling date squares
left over from the funerals
Why, I saw him only yesterday
It just goes to show you

Rooming House

1. In the Basement

The middle-aged
Ukrainian bachelor
has one room for his bed
stove, fridge, his
black and white TV

He used to farm
north of here on land
whose only purpose
was to hold the rocks
ice shouldered
to the surface every spring

Now he works nights
at the hospital
washes walls and floors
pushes his mop
up and down the halls

It's like moving
up and down the fields
he says, *no better*
no worse, same thoughts
go through your head

Every Friday
he knocks on my door
and gives me borscht
unless I've had a man
stay the night

then he won't speak
until I look guilty enough
for forgiveness
and more soup

2. Upstairs

He is ninety
but the only one
who has asked
for garden space
a narrow plot
behind the house

Early mornings
in the spring
he wakes me
his cane banging
down the stairs

Outside
in a John Deere cap
he sits in a chair
by his garden
watches the tender green
push through
thin, acidic soil

3. Across the Hall

The old woman's room
is smelly, cold and bare
a hot plate with one coil
burned out, a collapsible
metal cot, a hat box
with a feather hat
she says she wants
to leave me
A paralyzed cat
sleeps by the table
where she eats
her meal

Soon she'll give up
even these: windows
doors and ceiling lights
She'll move into
the four rooms
of the heart
Her cat will keep
the chambers clean
with his grey
fastidious
tongue

4. Main Floor Rooms

The lights go out
the coughing starts
I swear I'll move
to where I can't smell
onions and old age
or hear loneliness
drag itself
across the floor above me

Yet they hold me
these people who live
alone in rooms

As days grow longer
the space I live in
shrinks
until there will be
no place
left to go
            but here
where I am
right now

The Removal of Shoes

Their boots are found later
in front of the door
like old black dogs
waiting for morning
Their shoes
         in odd places
on top of the fridge
or lying like indolent cats
in patches of window sun

While those they loved
(if there were lovers or family)
prepared for sleep
             in different rooms
they sat on the edge
untied laces   or
undid straps
        narrow
across their ankles

By spring the old are found
in sweaters they knitted
beside them black purses
cracked from the cold
The young take shape
from melting snow
jackets or flannelette
nightgowns
            bright as flowers
to mark the place
where they decided to sleep
through a season   this
can be understood
when stories are told
as blizzards draw voices
around a fire   this
desire to walk
            into one's own death

but the removal of shoes

they placed them so neatly
where they could be found
                        before they opened doors
and stepped into snow

To Find Words

To find words
large enough to hold
the dead. Twenty-two young men
from the steel gang of the CPR
killed on highway number one.

My words cannot contain their lives.
I do not know their names,
the stories they liked to tell
after a hard day on the line,
the way they held their cigarettes,
the family pictures in their wallets.
I do not know them

can think of nothing
but the charred bodies
pulled from the wreck
and laid between blue lines
in the hockey rink

the only place in town
large and cold enough
to hold them.

Stillborn

who
looped the cord
around his fine new neck

who
hanged him
in my bone gallows   my

beautiful son
blue as the blue
in Chinese porcelain

Pariah

"For God sees how timid and beautiful you really are
and the thoughts of hope that go with you like little
white birds." — Malcolm Lowry, *Under the Volcano*

1.

The street dogs are turned
inside out, hair eaten by
ringworms, cameos of sores
pinned to their skin.
Lazarus dogs risen from
the nearly dead,
they wander the sidewalks
sniffing for food.

Three-legged, black
dugs hanging from its chest,
one cowers at our table,
never meets our eyes.

Lowest form of life,
pariah esta nada.

2.

At night they gather
courage in packs
we are told
they'll eat a child
or jump a man alone.

Do not swing a stick
the waiter says
*They will think
it is part of your arm
and eat their way up.
Bend as if you pick up stones,
these* perros *are not dumb,
they know stones.
They will melt into shadow.*

3.

In the early morning
before the sun has burned
clouds from the mountains
we drive to Chamula.
On the side of the road
a pariah lies on its back,
mouth locked open,
paws crossed on its breast
as if someone who cared
had placed them there.

As we drive by
a vulture hops away
like a toy on a spring
then hops back again.
Its beak sinks into the belly,
the anus, the hole that was an eye.

Lilies white, smooth as beeswax
grow in the ditch beside the dog.
The cups of their wide mouths
catch moisture from the clouds
like drops from weeping wounds.

Monologue: Prisoner Without a Name

Blindfolded,
you can't see who beats you.
It could be someone you called friend.
It could be your neighbour, or
the woman you saw buying bread,
the one who returned your smile
as she tapped the crust with her finger.

Sometimes there are voices far below
the pain. You hear about their children,
how one's son is failing school,
how another's daughter is growing beautiful.
You hear about the suppers that await them
in their houses on the other side
of town.

When all you have is pain and darkness
time stretches ahead like a desert
you can't walk out of, a desert
in a dream you cannot touch.
There is no reference point,
in two hours, tomorrow — these are things
you can't say, you don't know them anymore.

The first temptation is suicide,
then madness.

But one day you choose to survive.
You eat your food, the same food,
but you eat it differently.
You listen for rain on the roof, for wind.
You imagine wind in a woman's hair.
You sense when the one who beats you
is nervous
when he doesn't want to kill.

And so when you leave,
if they let you go,
there is something left of you
like a pebble you have hidden
all these months in your pocket,
a pebble you've polished in the darkness
behind the blindfold, bringing out its colours,
its shy designs.

And if you are lucky,
if this is a lucky stone, let's say,
you can push away the bitterness
and there is room for something else,
another feeling, perhaps something
close to love

Indigo

Three sounds beneath the mountain:
a stream over stones,
the clacking of looms,
the younger woman laughing.

She is sixty-five
and still an apprentice.
It may be years before
she takes the name of her teacher.
Or it may be tomorrow.
Her teacher is ninety.
Her hands know everything,
they move with the quickness
of wrens.

Outside the hut, the wind
has found a form to take.
It sways on the line,
long strips of bright
cotton. The evening settles
like a dove over the valley,
the looms are silent. One woman
stirs dye in a wooden vat.
The other carries cloth
to the mountain stream.

Every day the old one grows
in the other's eyes.
There is much to learn
and much to teach
here
where all things are:

the mountain,
the stream flowing from it,
two women at the centre,
all the blue of the world
flowing through their veins
into cloth
for those who live in cities
they have no need to see.

Rilke

He makes the words new again. Bright
as cutlery set for the evening meal
you've anticipated since waking.

When you pick them up
they fit into the hand
                              comfortably
as if a silversmith had studied
the palm's hollow, the length
of your fingers.

Full of possibilities
                    like spoons

how many different things
they can hold!

Time To Praise

In the morning
when the house is quiet
I sit at the table

contemplate
                the old stove
how it glows
in first light

nothing is more white
more sure of itself
even the sunlight

bends around it
here
against the kitchen wall

Even the Dead

Even the dead reach for you
as you walk, so beautiful,
across the earth.

Their fingers turn to flowers
as they break through
the soil, touch the air.

The bouquets in your room
are the hands of the dead,
transmuted. Roses.

Salal. Gladioli.
Scent covers you, a fine dust.
Leaves move in benediction.

Even the dead bless you.
Their blossoms glow
like muted lanterns

lighting your way
as you walk
green paths of sleep.

Stepping Stones

Let's catch minnows in a jar,
abandon our shoes on the bank
like an old sorrow, a heaviness.
Let's cross the creek
only for the sake of crossing
the slippery stones
which may or may not
hold our weight.

Though there's no time
to hesitate (all is in the movement,
the lack of pause) everything
at this moment
depends
on the firm and precise
placing of the
foot.

With Your Steps You Measure

With your steps you measure
the ground our house will fill
knowing both of us have done this
with other people, in other places.
But this is different, we aren't young,
love isn't easy anymore.

By the cornerpost I find a grouse.
I touch the feathered eyelids,
think of the soft sleep the bird
has fallen into. In another place
I'd call it death but here
it is silence, a sense of peace.

Is this why we've come,
for something so simple?
A broken windmill, a dugout,
cold water from a well.

The house we have imagined
builds itself around us.
Like the bodies of lovers
who have been together years
the boards find their places,
fit snugly one against the other.
Stories rise above the trees;
doors and windows that have opened
inside of us, open in the rooms
so all our empty spaces
fill with wind and light.

The THUNDER CREEK CO-OP is a production co-operative registered with the Saskatchewan Department of Co-operatives and Co-operative Development. It was formed to publish prairie writing — poetry, prose, songs and plays.

PUBLICATIONS

100% CRACKED WHEAT, an excellent source of dietary laughter from Saskatchewan writers, edited by Robert Currie, Gary Hyland, and Jim McLean, $3.95.

THE WEATHER, passionate, marvellous poems by Lorna Crozier, $6.00 pb, $14.00 hb.

THE BLUE POOLS OF PARADISE, a document of secrets, poems by Mick Burrs, $6.00 pb, $14.00 hb.

GOING PLACES, poems that take you on a vacation with Don Kerr, $6.00 pb, $14.00 hb.

GRINGO: POEMS AND JOURNALS FROM LATIN AMERICA by Dennis Gruending, $6.00 pb, $14.00 hb.

NIGHT GAMES, stories by Robert Currie, $7.00 pb, $15.00 hb.

SASKATCHEWAN GOLD, a powerful collection of short stories from the new west, edited by Geoffrey Ursell, $3.50.

THE SECRET LIFE OF RAILROADERS, the funniest poems ever to roll down the main line, by Jim McLean, $5.00.

EARTH DREAMS, startlingly original poems by Jerry Rush, $5.00.

BLACK POWDER: ESTEVAN, 1931, a play with music by Rex Deverell and Geoffrey Ursell, $5.00.

SINCLAIR ROSS: A READER'S GUIDE by Ken Mitchell. With two stories by Sinclair Ross, $7.00.

ALL STAR POET, hockey poems by Stephen Scriver, $2.95.

A NEW IMPROVED SKY, poems by Don Kerr, $5.00.

SUNDOGS, an anthology of the best in Saskatchewan short stories, edited by Robert Kroetsch, $7.95.

WILD MAN'S BUTTE, a dramatic poem set in Saskatchewan's Big Muddy, by Terrence Heath and Anne Szumigalski, $3.00.

SUPERWHEEL, the musical play about automobiles, with script by Rex Deverell and music and lyrics by Geoffrey Ursell, $5.00.

NUMBER ONE HARD, an L.P. of the songs by Geoffrey Ursell from the original Globe Theatre production, "an investigative documentary about the prairie grain industry," $6.00.

NUMBER ONE NORTHERN, an anthology of Saskatchewan poetry. Winner of the 1978 Saskatchewan Publishing Prize, $7.00.

EYE OF A STRANGER, poems by Garry Raddysh, $4.00.

ODPOEMS &, poems by E.F. Dyck, $4.00.

GHOST HOUSE, stories and poems by Lois Simmie, $3.00.

MOVING IN FROM PARADISE, poems by Mick Burrs, $3.00.

HOME STREET, poems by Gary Hyland, $2.00.

MOVING OUT, poems by Robert Currie, $2.00.

PRAIRIE GRASS, PRAIRIE SKY, an L.P. with songs by Rob Bryanton, Bob Evans, Glenn Koudelka, Connie Kaldor, and Geoffrey Ursell, $7.00.

All of the above may be ordered from

THUNDER CREEK CO-OP
Box 239, Sub #1
Moose Jaw, Saskatchewan
S6H 5V0

LORNA CROZIER lives in Regina. Her poems have appeared in many periodicals and anthologies and in five books, of which **THE WEATHER** is the most recent. She has just received the Saskatchewan Arts Board's Senior Artist's Award.

Lorna has helped many beginning writers with their work. She has taught several classes at the Summer School of the Arts at Fort San, Saskatchewan, and has served as a writer-in-residence in south-west Saskatchewan. She is an active member of the Saskatchewan Writers Guild and has served on its Colony Committee.

Recently, Lorna Crozier has also been heard on CBC's "Stereo Morning" as a reviewer. At the moment she is working on a collective play which will be produced at Regina's Globe Theatre early in 1984.